LITTLE GARDENS FOR BOYS AND GIRLS

BY

MARTA MARGARET HIGGINS

APPLEWOOD BOOKS

Bedford, Massachusetts

Little Gardens for Boys and Girls
was originally published in
1910

ISBN: 978-1-4290-9098-8

Prepared for publishing by HP

LITTLE GARDENS
FOR
BOYS AND GIRLS

AN EARLY FAILURE (*page* 3)

POSSIBILITIES (*page* 3)

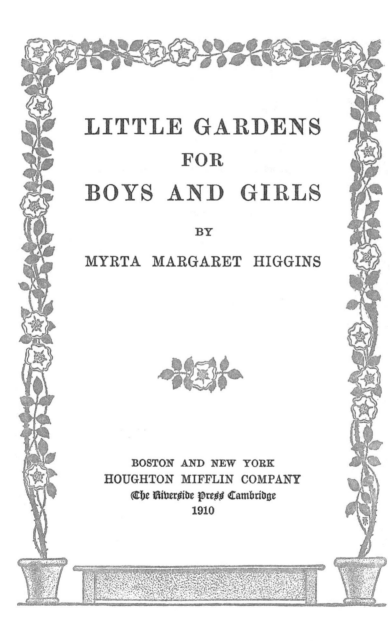

LITTLE GARDENS
FOR
BOYS AND GIRLS

BY

MYRTA MARGARET HIGGINS

BOSTON AND NEW YORK
HOUGHTON MIFFLIN COMPANY
The Riverside Press Cambridge
1910

TO THE BOYS AND GIRLS
WHO HAVE HELPED ME TO FIND
WHAT IS WORTH WHILE
IN A GARDEN

PREFACE

THIS little book has been written out of my own experience in trying to help hundreds of boys and girls to find the true value of gardening. It is written for the larger number of boys and girls who have neither greenhouses nor old established gardens, and I have hoped to answer some of the questions which I have been obliged to answer orally many times.

My aim has been twofold, — first, to make plain subjects that at first mention seem so simple they are seldom explained even in books for boys and girls, — such as the best way to take a weed out of the ground, or how a garden path should be cleaned; secondly, to arouse an interest in plant life that will be lasting and helpful.

This book is written in the hope that it may become a companion to the young gar-

PREFACE

dener and a guide to those who are trying
to help him. It does not claim to furnish ex-
tensive information on gardening, but rather
to give the right suggestion at the right
time and the inspiration for a further search
for garden knowledge and experiences. First
arousing interest in the larger world-garden,
and in the plant, which is the garden unit, it
begins with the fall months, when a garden
should be begun, and follows through the sea-
sons. If allowed to become a part of the garden experience year after year, the meaning
of its words will become clearer to the boy or
girl, for of necessity, and in order to lead them
into garden paths and the terms of a gardener, I have used some words which must
be turned over in the mind many times.

If the right point of view shall have been
attained by the young gardener, the purpose
of my book will have been fulfilled.

CONTENTS

I. The Great World-Garden 1

II. The Plant Story 17

III. Tools and Plans 29

IV. When and How to Begin 45

V. Autumn Work in the Garden 53

VI. The Garden in Winter and Indoor Gardening 63

VII. Garden Friends and a Dream Garden . . 73

VIII. Garden Handicraft 81

IX. The Preparation for Spring 89

X. Spring Work in the Garden 103

XI. Do Roses grow from Seed? 113

XII. Garden Helps and Hindrances . . . 121

XIII. Summer in the Garden 131

XIV. The Harvest 141

XV. In the Years to Come 149

ILLUSTRATIONS

An Early Failure ⎫
               ⎬ (*page 3*) . . . . *Frontispiece*
Possibilities ⎭

A Glimpse of the Great World-Garden 4

Before 12

After 12

A Young Gardener with her Tools 32

Facing down 32

Garden Plans 40–44

Diagram showing Depths and Distances for planting Bulbs 59

A Cold-Frame 61

Garden Stake 84

Markers 84

Sweet Alyssum 94

The Vegetable Garden 94

A Flower Garden just started 108

The Same Garden in Full Bloom 108

The Right Way to weed a Flower-Bed 134

Watering the Garden 134

A Trellis 137

The Reward of the Harvest 144

O world as God has made it! All is beauty.

BROWNING.

The very world, which is the world
Of all of us.

WORDSWORTH.

God gives us with our rugged soil
The power to make it Eden fair.

WHITTIER.

LITTLE GARDENS FOR BOYS AND GIRLS

CHAPTER I

THE GREAT WORLD-GARDEN

How happy are the faces of the children in the frontispiece of this little book! They are happy because they are learning to make gardens. Even the little girl who has failed to make a weed grow in a tin can is not discouraged, and the children hovering over the basket of flowers are happy as bees. It is a great delight to have a garden all one's own. Yet what seems to belong to ourselves alone is shared by many another. Not to the seedsman alone, but to many others also we owe our thanks for aid in making our garden Not to ourselves alone is all the pleasure and the profit.

3

LITTLE GARDENS

Even the passer-by shares in the joy of the bright colors. Together we have a common interest in the great world-garden about us, which supplies us with the material for all our gardens.

Let us look at that great world-garden and see what it means to us. An all-wise Gardener must have planned the great garden that spreads over the hills and valleys. If you go out into the fields and woods you see flowers blossoming that no man planted or tended, trees that no man cared for, making shelter for the birds, and cool, shady places for man and beast. There, too, is food for all the wild creatures.

It may seem to you that all these things have grown up without any plan or care, but if you look carefully, and learn what the past history of this earth tells us, you will see that our world-garden is developed along a most careful plan; that it is being planted and tended by winds and streams, storms and birds, and all the many forces

A GLIMPSE OF THE GREAT WORLD-GARDEN

and creatures of nature. Men who have studied
the face of the earth tell us of an ice age when
great rivers of ice flowing down over the land
crushed the great boulders of rock, grinding
them together until parts of them were made
into gravel and sand; and how the heat and
cold and the acid substances have cracked and
broken the stones, and the storms have swept
down upon the land, and washed the finely
ground sand in between the huge boulders and
made the fertile valleys, leaving the fine soil on
top and the coarse sand below to provide a good
drainage for the world-garden. A wonderful
life, both animal and vegetable, has sprung up
on this field of soil. For centuries men did
little with the wonderful forces that were in
their hands. Deserts remained deserts; dry
lands became drier. Only here and there crude
efforts were made to renew the land's fertility.
But with the dawn of our century of electricity

and science we began to watch and work for the possibilities that lie in this great earth of ours, and lo! we found that the desert could be made to bloom again and the dry land permanently watered, the barren soil renewed, the starved plants given new life, and the plant world made subject to man's use.

We are learning not to neglect our forests and waterways, our fields, and our friends of the animal world, but to care for them, protect and control them in such a way that nothing shall be wasted, but all made to serve its purpose in the great world-garden. Some men are working wonders in the plant world, creating new fruits and flowers that will be stronger and more useful than the old. Luther Burbank, whose name is of world-wide fame for his wonderful creations, has produced a cactus that is good food for man, and that can be raised on our own barren deserts where once we thought nothing of any

value would grow. Others are using the discov-
ered powers of the twentieth century to hold
back the rivers and turn them into the dry lands,
where they make the waste country bloom and
yield food for man. Still others are searching to
find out the use of birds and insects, and all the
other wonderful forms of life that exist in our
garden.

When we look about us we see that the places
which are not clean and beautiful are the result
of man's neglect or abuse. Now we each and all
can do our part to make and keep this world-
garden a place pleasant to live in, and a place
filled with good things. It is better for us to
begin by doing a little and doing it well. We
should be careful to help and not hinder, and
work with others in unity, so that a harmoni-
ous result shall be attained. Wherever we make
our own little garden, we should remember that
we must do nothing to mar the home-grounds

about us, but help to make them beautiful. We should remember that no matter where we live we have neighbors near or distant, we are a part of larger families, — the town or city family, the country family, the great world family. The interests of the fields, forests, and waterways are our interests; the interests of the parks and common grounds, and streets and buildings, are our interests; and the health, cleanliness, and beauty of our home city, town, or village directly concern and affect us for good or for evil.

Some day it may be the duty and privilege of many of us to help in forming a town or city, or to help in caring for streets and common grounds; and we are not too young to begin to think about such things now, and to look about us to see how such things are done. We like clean streets. Have the people provided boxes for waste paper and rubbish? Do the boys and girls help to keep the place clean by putting things in their proper places instead of scattering them? Look about the streets of your town. Which streets do you like best? The broad street shaded by beautiful street-trees where the homes are surrounded by green lawns, trees and shrubs, with flowers and vegetables in abundance. Are you helping to care for the trees on your street? Are you doing all you can to keep the lawn clean and green, and to protect the garden? When you visit parks and commons, do you remember that they belong partly to you and that they are to be enjoyed and not abused?

One of the problems to be met in every place is the disposal of ashes, refuse and rubbish. It is sometimes partly controlled by the town or city, sometimes partly controlled by an improvement society, and too often not properly controlled by any one. Refuse, if not used as food for animals, should be buried deeply away from buildings, or burned and then buried, or carried away and disposed of as the town may provide. Rubbish should be carefully stored in barrels or boxes and frequently hauled away. It should be dumped only in places that need to be filled in, and only when the owner of the land consents. The owner, or the Improvement Society, should see that such places are frequently covered with soil, or at least that small spots here and there are given a little soil and planted with vines such as the wild cucumber or the virgin's bower, so that the place will be covered, at least in summer. Wood ashes are excellent for lawn and garden, but coal ashes tend to harden the ground and are usually good only for filling in hollows. Ash barrels, garbage pails, and rubbish heaps can at least be protected and hidden by trellises and vines, just as clothes-lines and small buildings about the place are often cared for in such a way that the landscape is not made ugly by their presence. There is a way to dispose of everything so that nothing shall become a menace to health or an unsightly object.

What each one does toward making the world-garden more beautiful may be very little, but it all counts. It may be that some can have only a window-box, or a single plant, or a tub or a box of plants. Some may have a single tree or shrub to care for, while others may care for a whole lawn, grass, shrubs, trees and flowers, and walks. If you have a shady corner where many flowers will not grow, fill it with ferns from the dry woodland. Some people think they cannot have any flowers because they have only shady corners, but with ferns for a background you may have forget-me-nots and lilies-of-the-valley for early flowers, and fairy lilies and pansies for later bloom. The fairy lily is sometimes called zephyranthes or zephyr flower. It grows from a bulb, and its pink or white star-like blossom is very pretty among the ferns. There are other

11

flowers that bloom in the shade, but these are the prettiest, I think.

You need not fail to have flowers because of lack of plants or seeds, for if you live in the city seeds are inexpensive, and if you live in the country there are many wild flowers that will flourish in your gardens. What can be more beautiful than golden-rod in autumn and violets in the spring?

As I was saying, there is something for each of us to do to make the world-garden more beautiful, and some of us find very much to do. When the garden idea came to one boy he found that the small ground space around his home was almost as bare as the street. He made a lawn and a small flower bed near the house and in the corner of the fence. At the back of the house he planted vines to cover the fence and an old building, and where the coal ashes had been, he planted a vegetable garden which grew

BEFORE

AFTER

so well that you could hardly believe that he had had no fertilizer. How did he do it? He spaded and raked the soil very thoroughly. He planted carefully. He had no roller to roll his lawn, so he pressed it firmly with a board. He had no watering-can, or hose, or lawn mower. But he poured water on his lawn and borrowed a mower to mow it. All this was done in a place that had been bare for eight years. He kept his garden well weeded. It was small, but he reaped a harvest of vegetables and flowers. He had never done any gardening before, but was willing to ask advice and use it, and to learn from his own experience.

Many boys have raised vegetables for selling and have netted good sums for their labor. Hundreds of boys and girls are beginning to know the enjoyment that comes from reaping fresh vegetables and flowers raised by their own care. Some children living in tenements have

13

made good use of the only bit of land they had, which was under the clothes-lines. By hauling in soil and banking it with sod they made flower beds around three sides and a circular one in the centre, still leaving room to walk about under the lines. There is no spot where it is not possible to have a garden of some kind.

If you are going to make a flower bed or a garden, the first thing to do is to look about, and think and plan. So many boys and girls put the spade into the ground before they think, and wonder afterward why they met with failure. "Thought before Action" must be your garden motto. The first thing to think about is what you have to deal with, — namely, the plant. The soil, the air and water, and the plant food, all these and many other things will have to be reckoned with, but your means to your end and the centre of your interest is the plant. As you study the plant to find out how it lives and how

14

you can help it to become a useful and beautiful thing in your garden, remember that you are learning to do your part toward making and keeping the great world-garden a place both pleasant to live in and filled with good things.

II
THE PLANT STORY

Flower in the crannied wall,
I pluck you out of the crannies,
I hold you here, root and all, in my hand,
Little flower — but *if* I could understand
What you are, root and all, and all in all,
I should know what God and man is.

TENNYSON.

CHAPTER II

PULL a full-grown plant out of the ground. Here you have root, stem, leaf, flower, and perhaps partly developed fruit or seed; all this from the tiny green sprout you saw breaking its way up out of the ground a short time before. In order to grow it must have eaten. The root that held the plant in the ground searched for its food in the soil. The many rootlets tell you how diligently it searched. From these rootlets many short-lived hairs reached out, clung to the soil, and sucked its substance. The plant food must become liquid before the root can take it up, so you see the soil must be very fine, in order that the acid in the root and the water in the soil may dissolve the food in the tiny particles. The food is taken up the root and stem into the leaves, where it is spread to the air and sunshine. The leaves are the stomach of the plant. From the air, from water, and from the plant food that is brought up from the soil, they manufacture substances that can be assimilated or made over into parts of the growing plant body. Some of these substances are often stored in the root until a fruit or seed begins to form in the blossom, when they are needed there. Let a radish go to seed, and cut open the root. What has happened? The radish is beginning to look hollow. The food has been taken up to nourish the seed.

The flower of the plant may be formed in different ways, but you will find that nearly always it has an outer covering to protect the bud, called the *calyx;* then comes the *corolla,* which is usually the part we admire in our flowers, the expanding, showy part. The parts of the calyx are called *sepals,* and the parts of

20

the corolla are called *petals*. Inside are the *stamens*, holding *pollen* in their *anthers*, and in the centre of the flower is the *pistil*, usually a tiny knobbed stalk leading down to the very heart of the blossom, where it enlarges to form the little seed-case that will come to view when the petals fall. This may develop into a fruit like the apple, or the seed-cases may just harden and hold the seeds until they are ripe. Some of the flowers, such as the poppy and the china pink, form very pretty seed-boxes to hold the seeds. Some seeds fall directly to the ground, while others having feathery tufts are carried by the wind to a greater distance. The seeds of your plants are not less interesting than the showy flowers which came before them.

Now it may seem to you that all this has nothing to do with gardening, but I wished you to understand why you ought to make and keep a fine soft bed of soil, and to furnish plenty of water for those tiny rootlets. If you realize what the plant is trying to do, you will not let it die, unless by so doing it serves a high purpose. This little plant is trying to live forever, and it has in it that which would enable it to live, though its outer form might die many times.

A plant either grows a seed which, planted, will carry on the life within it; or it sends out, from root, stem, or leaf, another little plant to continue the life within. Some plants do this readily, while others have to be helped. A plant may die, or, we might say, change its outer form every year. If so, we call it an annual plant. If it continues two years, we call it a biennial. If it continues many years, we call it a perennial. Nasturtiums are annuals; hollyhocks and sweet Williams are biennials; peonies and roses are perennials. Lettuce is an annual; parsnips are biennials, though we use them before they develop the second year; rhubarb is perennial. Nowadays, plants have been so changed by cultivation that we often have both annual and perennial varieties of the same kind of plant, and biennials and perennials which formerly did not bloom the first year from seed are now developed so that they can be made to do so.

The plant needs to be kept clean, so that it can breathe through its pores, and, like us, needs plenty of water and good air as well as food to nourish it. Just as our bodies need food to make blood, bone, and muscle, so plants need their kind of food to produce the substances which make up leaf, flower, and fruit. Much of the plant's food is decayed animal or vegetable matter and pulverized mineral matter. So, you see, the world is so well planned that when a thing becomes apparently worthless it is food for another kind of life, and that life, in turn, feeds another form of life. How dependent each form

23

of life on another! How bound up together that which seems divided!

The kinds of food which our plants need may not be in the soil where we have chosen to have our garden, so if we wish a good growth we have to supply the lack in the form of special plant foods which we call fertilizers. When a chemist takes the soil and analyzes it he finds it contains nearly seventy elements. Only twelve of the seventy are essential to agriculture, however.

Four of these — nitrogen, phosphoric acid, potash and lime — are so much used by plant growth that sufficient quantities for the gardener's use are seldom found in the soil. They can be bought in different forms, as they are found in certain rocks, in bone and other materials, and are ground up for the gardener's use. They are sometimes combined in a fertilizer which is often called the commercial fertilizer. It is a study in itself to know just what fertilizers to

24

buy and how to apply them. You may be told that nitrogen is best for vegetables grown for leaf development, as lettuce and cabbage; potash for root growth and brilliant bloom; and that phosphoric acid produces seed and fruit.

Experiment as much as you like, but never forget that the best all-round fertilizer is a well-rotted stable manure, from a stable where horses, cows, and pigs are kept, as on a farm. Remember that though you should have this if you can get it, it is not impossible to make a little garden with a few pounds of commercial fertilizer, or without any at all; for there is always some plant food in the soil, and plenty of water and sunshine will do a great deal if you hoe your garden well, so that the little plant may get its food and the air and water it needs so much. Wood ashes are good for your plant, and waste water from the sink, which often contains some grease, has fed many a plant into better growth. Manure from the poultry-yard may be used, but not in large quantities unless combined with wood ashes.

As we have said, the plant food must finally become a liquid, and though we may help in this matter by giving water to our gardens, yet there is always more or less water in the soil. It comes in the form of rain, snow, hail, or dew. It sinks into the soil and covers the particles like a film.

The soil holds the food and water for the plant. A rock contains mineral food, but only small plants like mosses can grow upon it. When the processes of ages have worn the rock down to a fine sand, the food it contains more easily becomes liquid, and it supports more plant growth. Certain kinds of rock finely gound make a heavier soil than sand, which we call clay. Besides sand and clay, there is decayed animal and vegetable matter in the soil, which we call humus. We find humus in large quantities in the woods where leaves and other matter have decayed for years. The heavier soils hold more water, but they do not part with it as readily as sand. A good garden soil is a good mixture of sand, clay, and humus. The humus or organic matter contains the greatest amount of plant food.

There is something else in plant life that we ought to know about. Some time pull a few bean or pea plants out of the ground and examine the roots. It may be that you will find tiny knobs on the roots of the plants. These we call nodules. It takes a strong microscope and a man of science to tell you what they are. As far as we know they indicate the presence of bacteria, now considered to be a low form of vegetable life. The work that the tiny forms do for us is very wonderful. Nitrogen is a precious element much needed by the agriculturist, and it is the work of these bacteria to gather it from the air. The class of plants known as legumes (peas, etc.) encourage these bacteria to such an extent that they are often planted and ploughed under as a " green manure," where nitrogen is needed in the soil.

Thus man finds much to learn from the study of the plant and its ways of living. Time was when every plant was what we call wild, uncultivated and untrained. Man steps in, takes the wild fruits and makes them sweeter, cultivates the wild flowers and makes them larger. The inhabitants of our vegetable garden are the descendants of plants from all parts of the world, often much changed from the original plant. Let man cease to cultivate nature and soon all would run wild again. But man is not disposed to give up his kingship, and so he is making nature serve him and yield him ever increasing returns in the plant world.

III

TOOLS AND PLANS

Through cunning, with dibble, rake, mattock, and spade,
By line and by level trim garden is made.

TUSSER.

CHAPTER III

TOOLS AND PLANS

Tools do not make a garden. It is the will behind the tool that does the work, and it may be that one boy will do more with a stick than another with a whole set of tools. You need not be kept from gardening because you have no tools, for with the aid of a stick you can raise lettuce which, sold at four or five cents a head, will soon buy a hoe, and when you have a hoe you can raise beans which, sold at seven cents a quart, will soon give you money for a spading-fork, and when you have a hoe and a spading-fork, you have the most necessary tools for gardening. Remember that a spade, which resembles a flattened shovel, is different from the spading-fork, which has tines. The latter is much more useful in breaking up the ground.

31

LITTLE GARDENS

A rake, a trowel, and a weeder are the next most necessary tools for you to have. It pays to buy good tools. They last longer and do better work. It pays to keep your tools clean and to sharpen them once in a while. Better work more easily done is the result. It pays to have a good place for each tool and to see that it is always put in its place when you have finished using it. It always pays to keep things in order. Orderliness in outward things helps to keep an orderly mind, without which we are of little use in the world.

A knee-mat is a good thing for a gardener to have, because with it he is more inclined to take an easy position when working at his garden beds. The chapter on Garden Handicraft will give suggestions for making knee-mats.

Watering-cans are rather expensive for the amount of good they do. Pails can be used if you are careful to hold them down low when

A YOUNG GARDENER WITH HER TOOLS

FACING DOWN

pouring the water, so that the force of a stream will not wash away the soil. A tin pail with holes driven in the bottom might serve the purpose of a watering-can. There is a great deal in using tools so as to make them do their best work in the easiest way. Farther on I shall have more to say about watering and about the uses of the different tools.

Here are some good things to remember. When you start to do your gardening do not try elaborate schemes that never look well unless given elaborate care. Make simple plans. Keep flowers, shrubs, and trees for the most part near the boundaries, leaving the open space for lawn. Trees and shrubs make a background for the flowers. If planting near the house, vines or tall flowers come first, then masses of a lower growth, lastly the edgings. This we call facing down. The same idea may be used in planting near fences or walls. Cover the background with vines, shrubs or tall plants, then put in the plants of medium height, and last of all the edgings, just as trimming is put on a dress. Now you may have very little to do with all this, but it is well for you to know about it. In choosing the spot for your own little garden, if you have an opportunity for choice, don't try to make an elaborate flower bed on the centre of the lawn if there is any other place for it. If you wish to have vegetables or any flowers but the shade-loving ones, select a sunny spot. It would be a very good plan to have one tree and one shrub all your own to care for, not necessarily in your garden spot, but in a suitable place on the lawn.

If you intend to have a wild-flower garden always remember in bringing wild flowers to your home grounds that flowers growing in wet places cannot live if carried to dry places, and unless you have a wet ground to put them in

don't try to move them. Wild flowers growing
in shady woods must be put in shady corners.
If you wish wild flowers to grow in a sunny
place, get some from the open field.

Now for the plans. We have spoken of the
plan of the entire home grounds; next we shall
talk of the plans for your very own flower garden and vegetable plot, and of the general principles of garden planning.

You cannot make a plan for a garden until
you know where it is going to be. You must
know how much sun and shade it will have,
from what direction the sun will shine upon it
at noonday, what kind of soil it contains, and
how much space you have for it, also whether
it is to be alongside a fence or walk, against the
house, or in a large or small open space. When
you have decided where your garden will be
you should note all these things, and draw a plan
on paper or on the ground, before you do any

35

spading. Keep a plan on paper for future reference. Every place chosen for a garden should be suggestive of a plan to suit, but here are a few good suggestions as to method in planning.

If you have not learned to draw at school, you had better make a very simple plan, or let some one make it for you. If you know how to use a ruler, pencil and compass, and can combine circles, squares and oblongs, practice a while on paper and try different plans. When you lay out the garden you should have in place of the ruler a yard measure or a stick marked off by feet; in place of the pencil a pointed stick; and for a compass, a line and two stakes, one to swing around the other. If you are going to draw a plan on paper, let each foot of ground be represented by an inch, or you may take any other scale you choose.

In drawing garden plans you must remember that a design which is very good on paper may be a very poor plan for a garden. Keep your plans simple. Study the size and situation of your space and make the plan to fit it. Never make a bed so wide that you cannot reach the centre without stepping into it. Make paths not less than two feet nor more than four feet wide. Don't forget that if you are going to have a little flower garden or vegetable plot, it is safer and more cosy to fence it around. A wire fence may be used. Consider this part of your garden when drawing your plan. It will prove a support for vines. In planning a vegetable garden run your rows as nearly north and south as possible. Plant high growths such as corn at the north. Make beds for small things in a sunny situation, not behind the corn. Plant squashes and other vines only where they will have a chance to run.

As you study gardening more, you will become interested in the different forms of gardening. Nations show their individual characteristics in gardening, as in other arts. If there should be a world exhibition of gardens, where each nation planted a garden after its own manner, we could easily recognize the English garden with its bright-hued flower gardens inclosed by well - trimmed hedges; the Italian garden with its evergreen trees clipped into strange forms, its fountains, and its marble fittings; and the Japanese garden, a tiny world by itself, delightfully ordered from the stepping stones to the sunset tree; waterfall and lakelet, hillside and valley forming a miniature landscape. Here in America our gardens, like our cities, have been cosmopolitan, a combination of the gardens of all the other countries, a little of everything; but now, in our established independence, we are seeking in all things the "natural method," and so in gardening we are coming to a form of our own.

TOOLS AND PLANS

We are not trying to crowd a whole landscape into a small place, nor are we trying to make our out of doors look like a well-fitted drawing-room, however beautiful, but we are taking Nature as she is, and only making her look a little more abundant! In one word, "naturalization" is the keynote of our gardening to-day. We are planting the crocus and narcissus where they fall in the grass, the ferns under the apple trees, and the lilies in clumps by the wall. So much for garden principles and the gardens of other people! Now we can see better for ourselves.

Do not make a large garden the first year, because you cannot take care of much space until you have learned how, and when the weeding season comes you will become discouraged if your garden is more than you can care for. Here are a few plans and ideas that may help you.

LITTLE GARDENS

Although the general outline of your plan should be made in the fall, it may not be completely filled in until you select your seeds in preparation for the spring.

Flower beds for various places

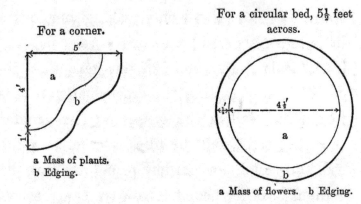

For a corner.

a Mass of plants.
b Edging.

For a circular bed, 5½ feet across.

a Mass of flowers.   b Edging.

For a border at the side of a lawn.

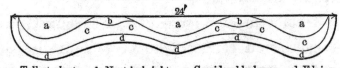

a Tallest plants.   b Next in height.   c Considerably lower.   d Edging.

A simple straight border along a walk.

a Mass of flowers.   b Edging.

40

A group of flower beds

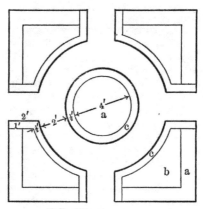

a Tallest flowers.
b Flowers of medium height.
c Edgings.

Radius of inner circle is 2 feet.

To make edging, increase radius $\frac{1}{2}$ foot.

To make path, again increase radius 2 feet.

To make second edging, again increase radius $\frac{1}{2}$ foot.

LITTLE GARDENS

A flower garden which may not be attempted the first year in its completeness, but beginning at the centre it may grow year after year with your experience

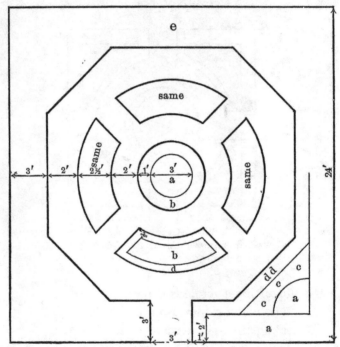

a Tallest plants.
b Plants of erect growth, but not extremely tall.
c Plants of fair height, more spreading growth.
d Edgings, rather stiff, as Dwarf French Marigold.
dd Edging, more branching, etc.
e A garden seat could be placed here.

TOOLS AND PLANS

An idea for a vegetable garden

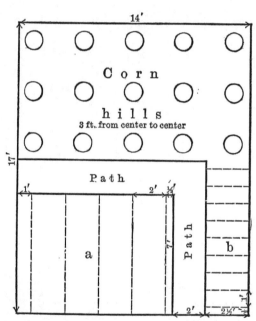

a Drills 2 feet apart for short vegetables, such as
  dwarf beans, beets, etc.
b Drills 1 foot apart; short rows, assuming they may
  be reached only from one side. Good for onions,
  lettuce, etc.

LITTLE GARDENS

A vegetable and flower garden combined

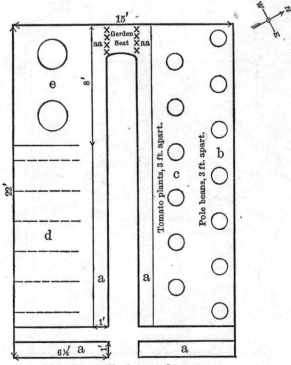

aa Vines over trellis above garden seat.
a Flowers.
b Tall plants, preferably pole beans.
c Lower, more spreading plants, preferably tomatoes.
d Drills, 2 feet apart, short growths.
e Hills of running vines, preferably summer squash.

44

IV

WHEN AND HOW TO BEGIN

A good beginning is half the battle.

PROVERB.

CHAPTER IV

You may begin a garden at any time of the year. There is always something you can do about it, but the best time for beginning, and the time that you should set aside for renewing your garden each year, is in the autumn, when the frost has killed the weakest plants, and the leaves begin to fall.

Select a sunny spot for your garden, if possible, for most flowers and vegetables are sun-loving plants. Select as good a soil as you can find in a sunny place. As we have said, there are sandy soils, and clay soils, and soils made up almost wholly of humus or decaying animal and vegetable matter, such as you find under trees in the woods, where a rich black soil is made from decaying leaves and roots. A good garden soil is the right combination of these three, — sand, clay, and humus. In color it is neither light as sand, gray like clay, nor black as humus, but it is brown, dark when wet, and light when dry.

Some boys and girls have no good soil in the place where they must have their garden, and they sometimes go to the woods or fields and bring in soil. If the place is wholly stone or gravel, it may be necessary to dig out or bank up a place to fill in with the new soil. Some boys and girls have only window or piazza boxes, or even boxes or tubs on the ground or roof. If you live in the country you will probably find plenty of good land, so that you need not carry any soil. If there should be none around your house, there are plenty of people willing to lend the use of land, if the privilege is not abused. If your place is sodded over, the sods should be taken out and put in some place where grass sod is needed, or piled up to rot and be used for a fertilizer later on. Save all the soil you can by shaking the sod, for this soil around the grass roots is fine for your garden.

When your ground has been selected, you should begin to measure and make your plans. See how much land you have, from which direction the sun shines at noon upon your garden, whether or not any shade falls upon it, and what is the general shape and situation of the spot you have chosen. Draw your plans, then with measure, line, and stake, lay them out on the ground. With a hoe make a slight trench in the ground under the lines you have drawn; or, by putting in a spading-fork and moving it a little back and forth, break the ground just at the edge all around your garden bed, so that when you spade, the ground will not break beyond the line. Clear the ground of all stone, rubbish, and weeds. The paths may be simply cleaned and made hard, or they may be filled in with gravel. Grass paths are very pretty, if well sodded, mowed, and kept trimmed.

If you have any manure, spread it on your ground now thickly enough to make a two-inch covering, and spade it in thoroughly. If you are going to use commercial fertilizer, wait until you are ready to plant, then scatter a thin coating over the surface of the bed or drill, and mix thoroughly with the soil. Whatever fertilizer you use should always be mixed thoroughly with the soil and forked in deep.

There are wrong and right ways of using tools. Learn to handle them lightly and effectively, and your gardening will be much more easily done. Learn the use of each kind of tool, and see how much you can do with it. We shall talk more about the use of the different kinds of tools as we go on.

WHEN AND HOW TO BEGIN

The best tool for breaking the ground is a spading-fork. When you are ready to spade, stand inside your plot facing one edge and having another edge close at your left side, so that your spading will always be from left to right as in writing. Put in your fork not more than ten or twelve inches from the edge, according to your strength and the size of your tool. Press it into the ground with your foot as straight and as far as you can. When you try to lift the soil, if it comes hard move your fork back and forth, break the ground a little, give another push, break again. You must finally lift up the forkful of soil, turn it over, and break up the lumps with the tines of your fork. Don't pack your soil. Keep it light and break it up as much as you can. When you throw the soil back in its place, leave a slight

51

trench just where you put your fork in, so that you can see when you take the next row just how far back you spaded. Don't leave an inch of ground unspaded.

Raking is the next process. Rake hard and deep, back and forth, to break up the lumps and shape your garden. When finished, a garden bed should be level on top, and not more than a few inches higher than the ground around it. A bed that is sloping and trenched around sheds the water like a roof, and is hard to care for and keep even. The only good reasons for ever making a bed up high are to get a greater depth of fine soil and good drainage in low land. Now that your garden bed is made, and your paths put in order, you are ready to do your first planting.

V

AUTUMN WORK IN THE GARDEN

The aster by the brook is dead,
    And quenched the golden-rod's brief fire,
The maple's last red leaf is shed,
    And dumb the birds' sweet choir.

．　　．　　．　　．　　．　　．　　．

The cricket is hoarse in the faded grass;
    The low brush rustles so thin and sere;
Swift overhead the small birds pass,
    With cries that are lonely and sweet and clear.
The last chill asters their petals fold
    And gone is the morning-glory's bell,
But close in a loving hand I hold
    Long sprays of the scarlet pimpernel,
And thick at my feet are blossom and leaf,
    Blossoms rich red as the robes of kings;
Hardly they 're touched by the autumn's grief;
    Do they surmise what the winter brings?

CELIA THAXTER.

CHAPTER V

AUTUMN WORK IN THE GARDEN

THE autumn is the best time of year to set out most trees, shrubs, and small perennial or biennial plants, and to separate plants that are too thickly grown. It is the time to plant many bulbs, such as tulip or crocus, and it is also a good time to sow many kinds of seed, such as poppy-seed, grass-seed, or spinach.

In setting out plants remember that the root is the important part, for it holds the plant in place, and it takes in the food and water for the plant, besides often acting as a storehouse for food. Cut the top from a plant and it may spring into life again, but cut off the root and it will surely die. Then give careful attention to the root. Dig a hole deep enough and broad enough for its rootlets to spread without being cramped. Put some manure into the hole, and mix it thoroughly with the soil. Hold up the plant in the hole to try it and see if the place is large enough, just as you would try a new suit to see if it fits. Work at it until it is just right, then set in the plant, carefully arranging its roots. Supporting it with one hand, carefully pack the earth closely about it. Give it a generous amount of water. If the soil should be very dry it is a good plan to fill the hole with water and let it soak into the ground before setting the plant. Never heap the soil about a plant; rather leave a circle of lower level than the ground about it to hold the water, except when winter is coming on; then the ground should be level about it so that the water will drain off and not form ice. When setting out small perennial or biennial plants, place them at one side of the garden where they may remain undisturbed for some time.

They may be set some distance apart and annuals may be grown between them. Foxgloves and larkspurs are two of the best perennials to have. The foxglove is very thrifty and a great attraction to bees. The larkspur is so superior to many flowers, one can hardly look on its heavenly blue and not be good.

Bulbs! There are bulbs and bulbs; hardy and tender; fall bulbs and spring bulbs; and there are tubers and corms, which you probably call bulbs. They are all underground stems. The tuber bears buds or "eyes" on its sides, like the potato; the corm is short, thick, and fleshy, and sends off roots from its lower face, like the crocus; the bulb consists of thickened scales or modified leaves, as in the onion. The important thing for you to learn about underground stems of this kind is whether to plant them in fall or spring, for the tender ones decay if left in the ground through the winter.

You can learn much by looking over a good bulb catalogue. Dahlia, canna, and gladiolus are spring bulbs; tulip, crocus, and jonquil are fall bulbs.

Arrange the bulbs on the surface of the ground just as you wish to plant them, or scatter them and plant them where they fall. Then take a stick or trowel, if you have not a dibble, which is the proper tool for this work, and plant each one where you have arranged for it to go. Be sure to put the root end down and the top up. Rules for depth and distance of planting can usually be found in the catalogue of bulbs. Plant tulips about five inches deep and five inches apart; larger bulbs deeper and usually farther apart. Bulbs should never be planted in a low place where water will settle; they need a well-drained bed. Often when planting in the grass it is a good plan to put a little sand in each hole first and a little fresh loam. Though bulbs do better for being enriched with manure, they should never be allowed to come into contact with it, as it causes them to decay. Bulbous plants usually blossom only a short time and make little display of foliage, therefore it is best to

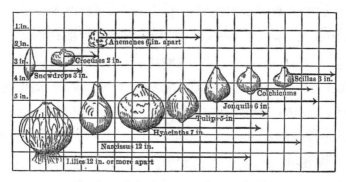

Depths and distances for planting bulbs.

By permission of J. Horace McFarland Co.

plant them in the grass or among other plants in the garden. Bulbs planted in the fall may be left in the ground the year round; but if they are removed to give place to something else, and are to be planted again, they should not be taken up until the foliage has ripened. The bulb you take up is not always the same bulb you planted, but a new one grown beside the old, which has given its life and is decayed. Some bulbs need more than one season's growth to make them large blooming bulbs.

Some seeds may be planted late in the fall, such as poppy-seeds in the flower garden, or spinach-seeds in the vegetable garden. Scatter them and rake them in, or plant in drills, which are like tiny furrows, and press the earth firmly over them.

When your fall plants, bulbs, and seeds are planted and the cold weather has come in good earnest, cover the beds with leaves and pine boughs, or something to keep them from blowing away. Oak or maple leaves are best. Never burn leaves. Pile them where they can decay or mix them with manure. In another year or so they will be good to enrich your soil.

AUTUMN WORK

It is a good plan in the autumn to carry a small box of earth into the cellar to use for winter or spring house-gardening. Autumn is the time to make a cold-frame or hotbed. Heavy planks sunk in the ground and slanting toward the south make the framework. Glass or cheese-cloth will complete the top. A cold-frame is filled with rich soil, but a hotbed has in addition a foundation of fresh horse-manure to provide heat. Have your frame ready in the fall. In the spring add the glass or cheese-cloth, and plant as soon as the condition of the soil permits.

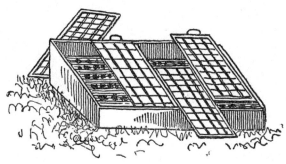

A cold-frame.

VI

THE GARDEN IN WINTER, AND INDOOR GARDENING

The speckled sky is dim with snow,
The light flakes falter and fall slow;
Athwart the hill-top, rapt and pale,
Silently drops a silvery veil;
And all the valley is shut in
By flickering curtains gray and thin.

But cheerily the chickadee
Singeth to me on fence and tree;
The snow sails round him as he sings,
White as the down of angels' wings.

I watch the slow flakes as they fall
On bank and brier and broken wall;
Over the orchard, waste and brown,
All noiselessly they settle down,
Tipping the apple-boughs, and each
Light quivering twig of plum and peach.

On turf and curb and bower-roof
The snow-storm spreads its ivory woof;
It paves with pearl the garden-walk
And lovingly round tattered stalk
And shivering stem its magic weaves
A mantle fair as lily-leaves.

JOHN TOWNSEND TROWBRIDGE.

CHAPTER VI

THE GARDEN IN WINTER, AND INDOOR GARDENING

SOME people think of a garden as affording only a few months' pleasure in flower and fruit, but we should learn to see that a garden's full value is not found until everything that enters into the life of it has become a part of our experience. The great world-garden presents studies all the year round, and we shall find this equally true of our own little garden. When our daily observation is centred on a spot to which we give our love and labor, we often find more knowledge and experience within its small boundaries than we should gain in many wanderings.

It may be that during the first winter your garden will contain only sleeping life; but the life is surely there. Many a brown toad is sleeping where he burrowed into the ground when the wintry weather approached. The plants themselves are settling into their beds and resting and waiting for spring sunshine. The insects and the weed-seeds are there and will show themselves in the warm weather, but I hope you have partly rid yourself of these troublesome things by spading your garden thoroughly and thus exposing them to the freezing weather.

A winter garden such as we may enjoy some day would contain choice evergreens, shrubs with bright berries, and trees beautiful in line and covering; but even now we may somewhere plant or find at least one tree to call our own, and if it has many seeds like the birch it will attract the birds; then you will have life indeed in your winter garden. You may further entice the birds by offering them special food and protection. Tie a piece of suet on the tree for food. Place a piece of tin or wire-netting, in the shape of an inverted tin pan, about the trunk of the tree several feet from the ground, in order to keep the cats from climbing after the birds. One of the best of our birds is the chickadee, who sometimes whistles the phœbe note. He wears a black cap and broad, dark cravat and a blue-gray coat.

The real garden is always out of doors, — and the great world-garden in winter is more beautiful and more abounding in life than any indoor garden can be. Nevertheless, windows full of bright leaves and blossoms are entertaining and make home cheery. One plant well-grown is better than a lot of scraggy ones; and when you have found how much interest may gather around a single plant you will care less about having a large number. You will be surprised to see how much you can do for one plant and how well it will repay your care.

It is best to keep your plants in unpainted flower-pots, but tin cans or wooden tubs will sometimes do if holes are made in the bottom for drainage. When potting a plant see that the flower-pot is thoroughly clean. Let it soak in water for several hours at least before using, so that when the plant is first set into it the moisture in the soil will not be taken up by the flower-pot. Always place a few pieces of broken flower-pot or other coarse material in the bottom for drainage, taking care not to cover the hole in the centre. Fill the pot with finely sifted soil well shaken down. For potting soil use one third good garden loam, a little sharp sand, and either leaf mould from the woods or old rotted stable-manure. Fresh horse-manure is always too heating. Hen-manure is strong, and should be used in small quantities only. The scrapings from grass sods are good. Well-rotted cow-manure, or well-mixed and rotted manure from a farm, is good. Bone-meal may be bought for a few cents a pound, and is all right, but be sure to get that which is finely ground.

Mix the parts together thoroughly. When the pot is filled, take out enough soil to make room for the roots of the plant. Set in the plant, carefully arranging the roots. Support it with one hand and put the soil in about it, pressing firmly. Water thoroughly, and keep from a hot sun until well rooted.

When a plant is well started in a pot, never water it until the soil looks dry, then give it an abundance. Stir the top soil about a plant occasionally, in order to let in the air and also to help the rootlets to find the food in the soil. When a plant is preparing to bloom, give it a little extra water and plant food, — a tea-

69

spoonful of fine bone-meal or bone-dust, or a little liquid manure. To make the latter, turn hot water over manure. After it has set a while, use the water which can be drained from it. It is possible to overfeed plants and thus make them weak.

The dust in a house is a great hindrance to plants. Protect them from it as much as possible. Like us, plants desire cleanliness, fresh air and good food. Smooth-leaved plants are much benefited by shower baths. If insects attack plants, use Ivory soap suds, much weakened, as a wash.

The air in our houses is usually too dry and dusty, and often too warm for plants, and they require more attention than when out of doors. They also need especial protection on very cold nights. If a double window is not used, the plants should be drawn away from the window, or protected in freezing weather. Fresh air should be let into the room daily, but in such a way that it will not blow directly on the plants. The window might be lowered at the top and the air allowed to pass in above them. The dryness of a heated room may be partially overcome by keeping a dish of water on the stove, radiator, or register.

Turn the plants in a window once or twice a week so that they will get the light on all sides and have an even growth. Cut back your plants in such a way that they will make a bushy, compact growth and have more surface for blooms.

The best place for house-plants in summer is on a sheltered piazza, or in a protected nook where the pots can rest on a board or stone or ashes, or on the saucer of the flower-pot. If placed directly on the ground, the roots creep through the drainage-hole and have to be torn away in the fall, and this injures the plant. If put into the ground, the roots spread so that it is hard to get them into shape again.

Re-potting will be necessary when the growth of the plant demands it, but a plant blooms better if a little crowded for root-room. Always make changes gradually in spring and fall. A scorching hot sun and a strong wind should be avoided. Most house-plants are increased by slips, and another chapter will explain how this work is done.

If a few winter-blooming bulbs, such as jonquils, are desired, put the bulbs into the pot in the fall and set them in a cool, dark place for several weeks. Bring gradually to the light and water them. They should also be watered when set away, but not again until very dry. Bulbs need rich soil, but should never come in contact with manure. Use a little sand about them for protection.

VII

GARDEN FRIENDS, AND A DREAM GARDEN

One seed for another to make an exchange
With fellowly neighborhood seemeth not strange.

TUSSER.

CHAPTER VII

GARDEN FRIENDS, AND A DREAM GARDEN

THERE is nothing in the world that makes strangers become friends more quickly than the discovery that each loves a garden. The exchange of ideas, plants, and plans is the delight of garden neighbors. We find many a garden friend, not only in a neighborly way, but also in the world of books, and the winter is the time to seek them out. Gardens have been loved and written about so long that there is no end to the delightful things we may find in old authors as well as new. Some of the books you may not care to read until you are older, but I fancy a peep into them even now would heighten your interest in your own little garden spot. The names of Parkinson, Gerard, Evelyn, and others, you will see again and again. When some of the old writers wrote about gardens, they made large volumes describing the peculiar medicinal qualities of plants in a way that is strange to our day, but not wholly without value, and certainly entertaining. These old garden-books were sometimes called " Herbals."

Very little has been written for boys and girls about gardening, because it is only within a hundred years or so that there has been a deep interest in children's gardens. Some time ago there was a lady in England who loved children and gardens, and wrote interestingly about them. Her name was Mrs. Ewing, and she wrote " Mary's Meadow," and " Letters from a Little Garden," and " Our Field." More books are being written for boys and girls nowadays, and some have been written about gardens, but only a few that you could enjoy.

GARDEN FRIENDS

Some of the newer books on gardening written for older people would interest you after a few years' experience. There are magazines and magazine articles that ought to help you now, and perhaps our best friend of all is Uncle Sam. The United States and the State Boards of Agriculture are searching for knowledge all the time, and the results of their searches are published in pamphlets for free distribution. If you write to the Boards of Agriculture telling on what subjects you are in need of information, whether insects, weeds, or any garden-subject, pamphlets will be sent to you. So you see we have plenty of garden friends to help us, and they are increasing all the time.

In this as in any subject of study it is a good habit to take one topic at a time, — for instance, the soil, plant food, or a single kind of plant, as the aster or the corn, — and see

77

how much you can find out about that one subject both by your own observation and by a pursuit of that subject on the library shelves.

Make a garden note-book. In one half write the name of every garden-book you read or look into, its author's name, any helpful notes you glean from it, and your opinion of it. In the other half keep a record of your own garden, plan, dates of planting and gathering of crops, kinds and varieties planted, etc.

As you read the different ideas of people who love gardens, you cannot resist dreaming a little in the wintry days when your garden is resting and waiting for spring sunshine, — dreaming of an ideal garden which would be all that you desire. A little garden with a dainty hedge about it and a swinging gate, a winding walk, and blossoms, blossoms everywhere, — the heavenly blue larkspurs and pure white madonna lilies, canterbury bells and spikes of foxglove attracting the bees, roses and lilies, pink and purple columbine, — all these and many more! In the shadiest corner a little garden-seat, where we may sit and enjoy the work of our own hands, and watch and listen for the little visitors that come to our garden, — the little brown toad, the happy bird, and all the flying and creeping things that we do not always see unless we sit thus and watch for them! Take with you to your garden-seat paper and pencil or paint and brush, and this will become a delight. Not that we are artists, but in trying to draw things we see more plainly, for we are seeking a clearer mind-picture of the things around us. And last of all, let us forever dream and work for better gardens, beautiful and useful, not for ourselves only, but for all who may enjoy them!

Do not awaken from this dream to say it

LITTLE GARDENS

never can be true; for as true as you and I are friends, where there's a will there's a way, and a dream is the very beginning of things that are going to be real some day.

VIII

GARDEN HANDICRAFT

Let all your things have their place; let each part of your business have its time.

FRANKLIN.

CHAPTER VIII

GARDEN HANDICRAFT

In the wintry days there is still something to do for your garden. It is the best time to make a hundred and one little things that will be useful later on. If you have practiced at sloyd, or can use carpenter's tools, and like to paint, with very little expense you may make many things. Sometimes, if you have a very definite plan of what you are going to make when you go to buy the wood, a carpenter can saw the pieces into just the right shape and lengths, and they will be all ready for you to put together. Use a dark green or soft gray-green paint. Bright colors spoil the harmony of the garden color-scheme. Very pretty gates, fences and seats can be made from rough, unbarked wood. This is called rustic work. Many small things

LITTLE GARDENS

can be made from material you already have. It is well to know how to make a finished article from good material, but it is also essential to be able to make the most of what you have at hand. Butter boxes and tubs, and other small wooden articles out of use, suggest many possibilities.

LIST WITH SUGGESTIONS FOR MAKING

1. *Garden Stakes and Line.* Make stakes about 1 foot long and 1 inch wide; make notches on both sides 1½ inches from top. Point lower end. Get ball of strong, brown cord that will not kink, to use with stakes. Round holes are made in each article when possible that they may be held together, or hung on a nail when not in use.

2. *Markers.* These are wooden labels on which are to be written names and notes of plants which are important. Make 3 sizes. Small, 3½x1 inch to attach to plants. Medium, 9x1 inch, to keep in ground during summer.

84

Large, 15x2 inches, to stand through winter. Paint these labels white, so that marking will show.

3. *Stakes for Plant Supports.* Make length and strength according to plants to be supported. Paint green.

4. *Cold-frame Covering.* The cold-frame may require extra covering on cold nights. Make tiny flat bundles of straw, and tie them together with raffia side by side so that they will form a mat.

5. *Knee-mat.* A knee-mat on which the gardener may rest his knees when working close to the flowers not only saves his clothes, but enables him to take an easier position. Though many things might be used for this, perhaps the easiest to make is such as might be made from straw sewed or tied with raffia, as is often done with cold-frame coverings. I have seen boys make good knee-mats from the coverings of tea-chests sewed with raffia.

6. *Garden Baskets.* If you have learned the simplest steps of basketry, why not fashion garden baskets? Make the gathering basket rather shallow, and put a high handle on it. Make a basket for carrying small tools.

7. *Trellises.* These may be made of wood, or wire, or

both. Make them along simple lines and according to the plant and situation.

8. *Window and Piazza Boxes.* Make about 1 foot deep and 1 foot wide, and as long as the place permits. Make holes in bottom for drainage. Paint. Tubs with drainage holes and painted green will serve for some needs.

9. *Arrangement for Care of Tools.* Arrange a place for every tool, and keep every tool in place when not in use.

10. *Fences. Garden Seats. Garden Gates.* These are prettiest when made of rough, unbarked wood, and are then called rustic. It is hardly wise to attempt them the first year of your garden, but keep them in mind and you will get ideas about them.

11. *Bird Trays.* Make box about 9x10 inches and 8 or 10 inches deep. Make drainage holes. Fill with earth except in centre, where a dish or bulb pot with cork in drainage hole is to be kept filled with water. Make strong wooden brackets on which it is to rest some distance from the ground, on a tree or strong pole erected for the purpose.

12. *Bird Houses.* Make from old wood or partly decayed limbs of trees, or paint green, and tack bits of evergreen on the top. Make the roof to slant downward over the hole, and make the hole near the top of the box leaving the depth for the nest. Ten inches is not too deep for most nests. Make hole according to size of bird to be invited: for chickadee, $1\frac{1}{4}$ inches; for bluebird, $1\frac{1}{2}$ inches.

IX

THE PREPARATION FOR SPRING

The snow still lay in the hollows,

. . . . . .

But the smile of the sun was kinder,
  The breath of the air was sweet;

. . . .

  There shall be spring again!

Worth all the waiting and watching,
  The woe that the winter wrought,
Was the passion of gratitude that shook
  My soul at the blissful thought!

Soft rain and flowers and sunshine,
  Sweet winds and brooding skies,
Quick-flitting birds to fill the air
  With clear, delicious cries;

Nearer and ever nearer
  Drawing with every day!
But a little longer to wait and watch
  'Neath skies so cold and gray.

CELIA THAXTER.

CHAPTER IX

THE PREPARATION FOR SPRING

In January you must begin to think of spring. You should send to a good seedsman for a seed-catalogue, because if you select your seeds at home, where you can take plenty of time to think of the needs of your garden and study the descriptions of the flowers and vegetables, you will make a better choice of seeds. The catalogue will also contain many helpful facts about gardening. If you order your seed from a large seedsman or buy directly from a large seed-store, you can often obtain pamphlets or books containing just the information you need. Perhaps you will buy your seed in penny packets at school. If so, it is best to buy only a few packets and save five cents to buy from a seedsman one packet of some kind of seed that cannot be bought in penny packets, or a flower of some special color, for most of the penny packets are mixed colors. It is well to buy white sweet alyssum, or some other white flower, which will aid you in harmonizing the medley of colors that is likely to come in your penny packets. Beginners often make the mistake of buying too much seed. A few seeds well planted and tended give more pleasure, and produce a better effect. Five or six packets of seed would be sufficient for most children's gardens the first year.

You will find in the catalogue that the plants are classified by the terms of which we have spoken,—annual, biennial, and perennial; also as hardy, half-hardy, and tender, according to their ability to endure frosts and cold weather. You will find, also, that each plant may have several names. Plants often have more than one common name. Thus the cornflower is also called blue-bottle and bachelor's button. Aside from their common names in all languages, plants are given scientific names. These scientific names are in Latin, and are used all over the world, so that no matter in what country or what language gardeners and botanists may speak, they have one name for a plant. That name may have different parts just as do ours, telling to what family we belong, and giving to us also particular names of our own. Every name has a meaning, and the name of a plant is often a key to some of its characteristics.

Look at the plan of your flower garden which you made in the fall and see what it calls for: — vines; tall, medium, or short growing plants; edgings; shade-loving or sun-loving plants; plants of upright, stately growth, or branching or clinging habits; flowers for cutting, or for a beautiful effect out of doors. On these points alone there is opportunity for years of study and enjoyment, and each season ought to bring you some new experience of value and the acquaintance of at least one more flower. A few suggestions only can be given here.

White sweet alyssum is the safest edging plant for a beginner. It blooms throughout the season, and is not easily killed by frost. As its color is white, it will not spoil the color harmony of any flower bed. It can be easily trimmed into shape, or if not trimmed is always graceful. It is easy to grow. Dwarf French marigolds make a good formal edging. California poppies are good in rocky soil or clambering over rocks, and grow well if given enough moisture at the start. If asters are desired only for cutting, grow them in rows like vegetables, at least a foot apart. If wanted partly for effect in the garden, set them two feet apart, and plant earlier blooming plants like

SWEET ALYSSUM

THE VEGETABLE GARDEN

verbenas between them, so that there will be some bloom in the bed through the summertime. Plants that are killed by the first frost, like balsams, may be planted among hardier ones, and in the fall those which die first may be removed to give way to the others.

We have been talking just now of those flowers raised from seed which die the same season, and are called annuals. The raising of perennial plants from seed, and the care of plants raised in other ways, will be considered later on.

There are so many varieties of flowers nowadays that experience alone can tell you how to make a good combination in a flower bed, but these ideas may help you : —

First grouping. African Marigolds, edged with Dwarf French Marigolds; combined with Cornflowers, edged with Mignonette.

95

Second grouping (*for a single bed*).	Petunias (mixed), edged with Sweet Alyssum.
Third grouping (*for a border*).	Running Nasturtium, background. Coreopsis, mass. Dwarf Nasturtium, edging.

As for vegetables, some are excellent food, while others have little food value. Peas and shell beans have a high food value. If you wish to have wax beans get a variety that is stringless, fleshy, and not prone to rust. Plan to have a rotation of crops, that is, when an early crop has ripened put a later one in its place. It is better to follow a crop with one of a wholly different kind, which will take from the ground a different kind of food; for instance, a vegetable grown for leaf development, as lettuce, should be followed by pod-bearing or root crops. Turnips are not very valuable, but they are an easy late crop as they develop quickly. If you have a small amount of room always plant radishes at the same time with lettuce, and having the lettuce drills at least one foot apart plant the radishes halfway between them. The radishes grow quickly, and when pulled leave room for the cultivation of the lettuce. Some vegetables, such as tomatoes and celery, require such a long season that they are usually started in cold-frames or hotbeds. Certain vegetables require special culture and the right kind of soil, so that it is not wise to try to grow them without a knowledge of their needs.

PLANTS FOR BOYS AND GIRLS TO RAISE FROM SEED

FLOWERS

	ANNUALS	PERENNIALS AND BIENNIALS
Edgings	Sweet Alyssum. Candytuft. Dwarf Nasturtium. Dwarf French Marigold. Mignonette. California Poppy.	China Pink.

97

LITTLE GARDENS

	ANNUALS	PERENNIALS AND BIENNIALS
Medium Height	Petunia. Phlox Drummondi. Calendula. Verbena.	Sweet William.
Taller	African Marigold. Zinnia. Aster. Cornflower. Coreopsis. } Slender.	Foxglove. Larkspur. Hollyhock.
Vines	Nasturtium. Morning Glory. Scarlet Runner Bean. Wild Cucumber.	

VEGETABLES

SHORT	TALL	VINES
Beans.	Corn.	Pumpkins.
Beets.	Pole Beans.	Squash.
Carrots.		Cucumbers.
Parsley.		
Lettuce.		
Radishes.		
Onions.		
Potatoes.		
Spinach.		

PREPARATION FOR SPRING

SHORT

Turnips.

Tomatoes. ⎫
Peas.   ⎬ Require support.

Starting seedlings under the protection of cheese-cloth or glass is a good plan if well done. If not done well, it had better not be attempted, for a strong plant from a seed planted late in the ground gets ahead of a weak seedling started early, half-cared for, and not transplanted properly. The fact is that special care must be given to house-plants and seedlings, for Mother Nature does much for the outdoor plant for which we do not always give her full credit. If you wish to try early seedlings, however, salvia and asters are all right for flowers and tomato plants for vegetables. If you intend to sell the vegetables or flowers, remember that as the early bird gets the worm so the early marketman gets the high price. If you can raise seedlings well, and so get ahead of the season

99

with your vegetables and flowers, so much the better!

Seedlings may be raised in a cold-frame or a hotbed, which should have been started in the fall as told in the chapter on Autumn Work in the Garden. Radish and lettuce may be raised and matured in these without transplanting. The glass may have to be partly lifted or protected on hot days late in the spring.

In starting seedlings the two essential points to remember are, — first, to maintain the right amount of moisture; second, to maintain the right temperature in the soil. Seeds, if kept too wet, may mould. If allowed to become hot and dry at times the little plant after starting may die. Seedlings may be started in many different ways if moisture and temperature are carefully regulated. Grass sods may be taken into the house, placed in a box upside down, and seeds planted in them. They may be planted in eggshells, in strawberry baskets, or in small boxes having coarse material in the bottom with holes made for drainage.

A good garden loam is all right for starting seedlings. Do not let fertilizer or manure come in contact with the seed. If seeds are hard to germinate or sprout they may be placed in a box or flower-pot near the kitchen range to insure plenty of heat. In order to keep them moist also, place a piece of paper over the soil and keep it wet. As soon as the seedlings start into growth they need not only heat and moisture, but sunlight also. Whatever is used for starting them, remember it is important to have them in something that can either be broken apart or set in the ground, as sods, so that the little roots will not be disturbed. Paper flower-pots may be bought at the seed-stores, and these may be removed easily, leaving the little ball of roots unhurt.

The day of transplanting them into the ground is an important one. If the roots are torn the plant suffers a shock from which it will not speedily recover. Thoroughly water the little plant about half an hour before removing it. Prepare the places and fill them with water. Lift and set the plants, carefully arranging the roots. Shelter them from a hot sun for a week, but uncover them at night so they may receive the dew. Water them twice a day. A strawberry-box if high enough is a good covering for plants just set out. It lets the air in at the corners. Paper tents may be made and fastened down at the corners with stakes or stones or lumps of earth. Do not set seedlings into the ground until all danger from frost is past, and do it in dull weather if possible.

X

SPRING WORK IN THE GARDEN

This rule in gardening ne'er forget,
To sow dry and set wet.

PROVERB.

CHAPTER X

WHEN the birds come in numbers and begin to sing their songs we are sure that spring has come. Wake up your brown bulbs now. Uncover them a little each day. The winds of March sweep the earth and April's showers wash it, but still a rake with a boy behind it can reach the corners and crevices, and make the place look cleaner. Fallen leaves are excellent for mixing with the soil after they have decayed, but they should be gathered together for this purpose. Leaves lying about on the ground harbor the nests of insects. Take the leaves to the compost heap!

What is the compost heap? It is what will make your garden grow, — decaying leaves and sods, bones, any greasy substances from the

105

cooking kettles, manure, if you have it, lime, all mixed together and allowed to decay until the day your garden needs an extra dose.

Another good recipe for weak plants is liquid manure. Get a tub or barrel. Put manure in the bottom. Fill with water. Drain or dip off the water, and pour it about the roots of your plants. Be careful not to put it on the tops as it might burn them. Why is this any better than manure put into the ground? Do you remember in the Plant Story that we said the rootlets sucked in the food through tiny hair-like tubes, and that therefore their food must be taken in a liquid form? Then you see why this liquid manure can be taken in more quickly.

When the ground is warm and dry spade your garden again as in the fall. You do not gain anything by spading and planting while the ground is wet and cold. It does not break up nicely, but lies in lumps, and it is wise to wait for the right conditions.

Again rake your garden thoroughly. Use stake and line to make the edges neat and even.

In planting seed remember two rules : First, for depth of planting, about three times the size of the seed. Second, for distance of planting, according to future growth of the plant. Some seeds are scattered, some sown in hills, and some in drills. Poppy-seed is often scattered on the bed and raked in. Grass-seed is scattered, then raked and pressed into the ground. Sweet corn is planted in hills. This does not mean that the ground is heaped up at the beginning of the season, though it may be in the fall by reason of the hoeing. It means that small circular beds are planted at equal distances, and the corn instead of standing in drills is in groups of four or five stalks each. Parsnip, carrot and many other seeds are planted in drills, which are like tiny furrows. In drills there may be more than one line of seed. It is a good plan to sow them alternately in two lines. When you have had more experience you can scatter them along the drill, but not too thickly. That is the danger with young gardeners, — sowing seed too thickly. Because the seed is small do not forget the size of the plant. Even if you intend to " thin out " your plants, they will be injured if sown too thickly. All seeds should have the ground pressed firmly about them. The soil holds the food, moisture, and warmth for the little plant, and we are helping it to come close to its needs when we press the ground around it. Seeds must have the right amount of heat, moisture, and air in order to sprout. When the plant begins to grow, it must have light and food besides. The plant just beginning to grow has within the seed-case a small amount of food to give it a start. Cut open a bean that is partly

A FLOWER-GARDEN JUST STARTED

THE SAME GARDEN IN FULL BLOOM

sprouted. Find the tiny plant and the starchy food about it for it to feed upon. After this store is used up, the plant must obtain food from the soil in which you have placed it.

In order to sprout, seeds must have the right amount of heat and moisture. If too wet, they may decay. If allowed to become dry, the little sprout may die. If the spring should prove to be a very rainy one you cannot help conditions, but if dry and hot you can water your seedlings twice a day and protect them from a hot midday sun with newspapers for a few days. If you use fertilizer, be careful not to let it come in contact with the seed, but mix it thoroughly with the soil.

It is pretty safe to plant seed when the leaves have started out on the trees. Peas, both for flowers and for vegetables, may be planted earlier. In fact, they are about the first seeds to be planted in the spring. The peas should be sown in rather deep drills, but covered only the ordinary depth. As they grow, the earth can be gradually put about them to help support their weak vines and to give the roots a greater covering and a stronger foothold.

Young plants must be watched and cared for, or they will grow too thickly or be killed out by weeds and insects. In thinning out plants it is best to choose a time when the ground is wet, so that the roots of all the plants will not be disturbed as they will be if you do it when the soil is dry. In order to save your plants from disturbance place your left hand nearly flat upon the ground, letting the stem of the plant you wish to save come between your index and middle fingers, but not grasping the stem, while you pull out the other plant with your right hand. If your extra plants are weak and worthless, throw them away; but if they are good strong plants, and

110

the roots are not broken, either set them in another place or give them away.

This brings us to the question of transplanting, — which is a very important one. In the first place, do not keep plants out of the ground any longer than you can help. Have a place all ready for them if possible. If they cannot be set immediately, place damp soil over their roots and protect them from the sunshine. A cloudy day, when the ground is wet, is best for transplanting. Decide upon the arrangement for your plants, then make all the holes, and make them large enough to place in the roots without cramping. Fill the holes with water, unless the ground is very wet, and let it settle. Set each plant carefully, and support it with the left hand while you pack the earth about it with the right. Press the earth firmly at the last, and see that the plant is erect. Protect it from a hot sun for a week or more with strawberry-boxes or news-paper tents, give it water twice a day unless it rains, and uncover it to the dew at night.

The ground should not be disturbed where young seedlings are just coming up; but if they are in definite lines you can safely pull everything between and even risk a few seed-lings, rather than let the weeds get a start.

One word about veranda and window boxes. They are splendid if well cared for. The box should be about ten inches deep and one foot wide. It should be filled with good garden soil. Plants raised in a box need more water than in a garden, because the soil dries more quickly. Geraniums, fuchsias, petunias, and moneywort are perhaps the flowers most easily grown in a window or veranda box.

XI

DO ROSES GROW FROM SEED?

The lily has an air,
　　And the snowdrop a grace,
And the sweet pea a way,
　　And the heart's-ease a face,
Yet there's nothing like the rose
　　When she blows.

CHRISTINA G. ROSSETTI.

CHAPTER XI

DO ROSES GROW FROM SEED?

"Do roses grow from seed?" This was the question of a very little girl who loved flowers and unknowingly shared the opinion of all flower-lovers when she said, "I love roses." Yes, roses may be grown from seed, but they are oftener started by means of cuttings. This brings us to the question of how to increase plants in other ways than by sowing the seed. In the chapter on Indoor Gardening we spoke of increasing our plants by "slips," which are green or soft cuttings. Propagation is the word used by gardeners in speaking of the increase of plants whether by seed or cutting.

The little girl who loved the roses very wisely said, "I haven't learned to grow them yet." She did not know that very few people have learned to grow roses, nor did she know that more people, even boys and girls, might start roses and grow them if they wished to give them the necessary care. Really, the care of cuttings is not much harder than the starting of seedlings. People often fail in this and count it an ordinary loss!

A cutting from a rosebush should be taken from the part that is neither such old wood that it will not root readily, nor so green that it will be weak and liable to decay. Make a clear cut with a sharp knife below a joint and secure a piece having two or three joints. Leave only a few leaves upon it. Fill a flower-pot or box with sharp sand. Make a hole. Place the cutting in it, and press the sand around it so that one or two joints will be covered. The sand must not be allowed to become dry, neither must it be kept too wet. It must not be placed in the hot sunshine until

116

the little plant has begun to grow. Plants so started are not strong enough to be wintered the first season out of doors without protection, but if set out during the summer or early fall months, so that the young roots get a good hold before cold weather, and protected with earth and leaves, they may stand the winter. They could be kept in a cold-frame packed with leaves and perhaps with manure about the sides.

There are different kinds of cuttings. When we plant potatoes we make cuttings of the tubers, being careful to have one or two " eyes " in each piece, for that is where the sprout starts. Cuttings may be started by being inserted beneath the bark of another and stronger plant, as apple trees are started ; then they are called " grafts." There is an interesting way of starting plants called " layering." This method is often used with carnations. Instead of cutting a piece entirely off, a sharp cut is made just below a joint, but a bit of the stem is left uncut. The cut part is bent down and covered with earth except for a few inches, and the roots form there while the " slip " is still receiving some strength from the parent plant.

Do not be afraid to experiment with cuttings even if you lose them all the first time. It is fun to have a tiny nursery of cuttings, — a box of sharp sand in a protected place where they will receive good light and air, but not hot sunshine. Roots usually are well started in a few weeks, and the cuttings may then be carefully set into soil, but they must be watered and carefully tended. Hardy chrysanthemums are easily started in this way, and are splendid plants to own because of the lovely bloom they give us in the late fall.

When people are trimming their plants they are quite willing to give away cuttings. The kind of plants that are started by means of cuttings require much the same care as other plants, only they need more pruning, which is the term gardeners use for trimming. In pruning a tree or shrub, cut away all old wood, and the numerous small shoots which start about the base and which are called suckers because they take the life from the old plant. When a tree or shrub is in a dormant condition, — i. e., is not bearing developed buds, flowers, or fruit, — cut away a part of last year's growth evenly throughout, so that the future growth will not be too thick and thus weakened, but that the sunshine and air may reach all the parts.

XII

GARDEN HELPS AND HINDRANCES

I value my garden more for being full of blackbirds than of cherries, and very frankly give them fruit for their songs.

ADDISON.

CHAPTER XII

GARDEN HELPS AND HINDRANCES

PETS and babies, — babies of all kinds, — hens and chickens, cats and kittens, dogs and puppies, rabbits and all the rest, threaten the doom of our garden. In fact, it seems as if all the lovable creatures of the animal world were our enemies in the garden, because their wide-awake time is spent mostly in eating and playing. What is the remedy?

Nothing but the fence for most of them. Fence them in or fence them out, and give them a plenty of food and play elsewhere. If you protect your garden, when it is first coming up, by spreading brush over it, it may be able to stand by itself later on, but a fence or a hedge is a great protection. What of the little brothers and sisters who like to play at gardening and in the garden, and with or without mischievous intent make trouble for us? We cannot so easily fence them about! Then teach them to make play gardens of their own, — with sand and stones, sticks and weeds, show them how to make a little play garden.

There are tiny creatures that we cannot fence out, for they fly over the fence or crawl under through subways of their own making. Lady Butterfly, Madame Dragon-fly, and all the winged creatures, Mr. Caterpillar, Master Cutworm, and all their crawling neighbors, come to visit us. Ah! but some of these are our friends, and we would not fence them out if we could.

In time we shall find out our friends from our foes. The butterflies and bees are friendly, though some butterflies and moths lay eggs from which come dangerous enemies. The cutworm is an enemy, and his mother is a night-flying moth. If we put paper collars about our larger plants we may sometimes save them from being destroyed. Tobacco dust, chalk lines, or ashes will sometimes prevent an enemy from reaching the plant. If you see a plant lying on the ground with its stalk cut, you should dig in carefully near the surface of the ground for the cutworm, who is usually greenish brown in color. He must be taken out and killed. A wilting aster is often found to be troubled at the roots by ants or grubs.

The insects that trouble the gardener are treated according to the ways in which they eat. Some chew the plant; others suck the juices from it. The former can be killed by poisons on the plant which they will eat; the latter must be killed by contact poisons, or those that, touching their bodies, will suffocate them. There are many insect poisons on the market, and any seedsman can tell you which are needed for the kind of insect that troubles you, but most of them are dangerous to man, and it is often best to use simpler remedies. Sometimes a heavy spray of clear water will wash off the insects. Sometimes they can be knocked off and gathered in a can of kerosene. Ivory soapsuds cooled and weakened is often effective ; kerosene may be added to it.

Then there are the birds, most of them our friends, — yes, all of them if we are not stingy with them. Even the crow eats grubs as well as corn, and the rose-breasted grosbeak takes the potato-beetles, though he does steal a few peas. The birds are of such great assistance in ridding us of insect pests, we should protect them as much as possible. In every garden should be a bird-tray, erected some distance above the ground. In the tray and about the support plant vines, — morning-glory for the support and moneywort for the box. Petunias may also flourish in the box. Food may be scattered about, or tied to the tree or post. A dish in the centre of the tray should be kept clean and filled with water. Sometimes a flower-pot saucer, or shallow dish, filled with water, and partly hidden among the flowers, is used as a bathtub by the birds. Twine, feathers, moss and other material used in the making of nests may be placed near the tray for the use of the birds. Bird-houses should also be erected. The making of bird-houses and bird-trays is explained in the chapter on Garden Handicraft.

Last of all, let us talk of him who reigns King of the Garden. He with the bright eye, the quick tongue, — if he could talk, I 'm sure he would be witty! He of the brown coat and pale yellow waistcoat, sturdy and harmless, helpful and true! May we never harm him! And if perchance we happen to turn him suddenly from his resting-place in the ground, let us not frighten him, but gently move away and give him time to see what has happened.

Ah, Mr. Toad, you are my friend indeed! Only the other day an aster in my garden was dying. A large white grub was found at the root. I was about to move him out to the hard ground to kill him, when from somewhere among the leaves came Mr. Toad with a hoppity hop! Mr. Grub began to put his head to the ground and burrow again to hide himself. Mr. Toad saw the necessity for haste, and hoppity hop, gulp, gulp, gulp! Oh, what a swallow! Well, my trouble was over, the aster plant rescued, Mr. Toad my protector. And he is forever catching flies and other insects. He likes a cool shelter from the hot midday sun; an overturned box or a flower-pot with a slight excavation near one side will make it possible for him to stay in your garden.

An aquarium or basin of water is a fine thing

to have in your garden, but it is difficult to keep it clean. However, the toad will assist you in this matter if you will put in the basin some stones just reaching the surface of the water so that he may hop on them. A dish of water may be used and cleaned often, but a permanent aquarium should be made of cement.

With whatever kind of life we may be dealing, let us remember this, never fear, nor make afraid. Fear never did any good in the world. It makes a coward of you to be afraid. It hurts you to make another life have fear. You may think it does not hurt you to tease and frighten creatures. But it does n't harm the creature half so much as it harms you. It hurts the little boy or girl inside, and when you are grown up you may find it out some day. So kill mercifully when you must kill, and try to find some good use for all life. If an insect must be killed, put it on a hard place and kill it quickly.

XIII

SUMMER IN THE GARDEN

And hushed is the roar of the bitter north
  Before the might of Spring,
And up the frozen slope of the world
  Climbs Summer, triumphing.

Storm the earth with odors sweet,
  O ye flowers, that blaze in light!
Crowd about June's shining feet,
  All ye blossoms bright.

O the fragrance of the air
  With the breathing of the flowers!

CELIA THAXTER.

CHAPTER XIII

SUMMER IN THE GARDEN

THE first part of summer in a garden is tedious, — the hardest part of the garden year ; but the harvest soon follows, and we are rewarded according to our faithfulness. If you keep a garden thoroughly weeded and in first-class condition until the first or middle of July it is little trouble after that, and if you wish for a week's vacation, you can then leave your garden for a few days and not much harm will come.

Perhaps you think the greatest problem in your garden now is how to deal with the weeds. It *is* a problem, but easily solved. Be observant. When your plants first appear then come the weeds also, but if you have planted in straight rows, you are safe in destroying everything

133

between them. If you have not planted in rows, or if weeds are badly mixed with your plants, discover which are your plants by noticing the leaves. This may not be easy the first year of your garden unless you can get some one to tell you, but if you watch carefully you will soon know all the common weeds. The first two leaves of a plant are often very different from those that follow, but you will learn these differences in a little time with patience.

You should keep the soil stirred between your plants after they are started so that the weeds will never grow. There ought never to be any weeds large enough to pull, for a stick, or a weeder, or a small hoe or rake, will destroy all tiny sprouting weeds; but if a weed has mastered you so that it must be pulled, then grasp it near the root and do not break it off, for it will grow again. If the weed is near a plant, place one hand firmly on the ground

THE RIGHT WAY TO WEED A FLOWER-BED

WATERING THE GARDEN

about your plant so that the soil will not be moved, and pull the weed with the other hand at one side. There are a few weeds so strong of root that pulling is not enough without prying. Take a trowel, or a fork, and work it well down by the root, being careful to put in the tool straight and not slanting, so that it will not cut off the root. Lift, pry, and pull the weed until you have root and all. The point of a hoe is often more effective than the full edge of the blade when weeding.

Not only should your garden beds be free of weeds, but no weeds should be allowed to grow about your garden. The paths should be kept clean. In cleaning a path start at one end with the weeds and path ahead of you, not behind. First take out each weed with the point of your hoe. Then rake and level your path.

Watering is always a problem in the garden. In the first place, you will find that a good gardener does not always depend upon a daily watering except in drought, though of course water is what makes a garden look so refreshing in summer, and it is welcomed by most plants in large quantities in the summer time. What is more necessary than water is the constant stirring of the soil, — a shallow hoeing. Learn to use a hoe lightly and effectively. If the soil is allowed to become hard tiny holes can be seen on its surface. These are little water-ways, and the water that is down in the soil is coming up to the air and sunshine. Break up these water-ways with a light hoeing and the water must stay in the soil where it is needed by the roots. The moisture is often kept in the ground in hot weather by laying grass cuttings about the plants. This is called mulching.

The neatness and thriftiness of a garden in summer depend much upon careful training and trimming of plants. Some plants need

stakes, some need trellises. Plants like tomatoes, if not given support, should have plenty
of grass cuttings thrown on the
ground about them in order that
the fruit may not rot on the
ground. Peas should always have
support, for they bear better, and
in damp weather mould if allowed to lie on the ground. If
pea brush cannot be obtained,
buy wire netting, which will last
for some time if preserved from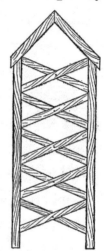
the weather when not in use. Many little an-
nual plants, especially petunias, do better for
being cut back.

When stirring the soil in summer, if a little
fertilizer is added the plants will do better.

August is the time to start plants for the
winter garden. Potting and repotting should
be done now, so that the plants will be well

started when taken into the house. Some garden plants bloom well in winter if potted now and cut back very closely. Petunias and salvias are easily grown, and are good bloomers in the house.

The starting of perennial and biennial plants from seed is often done at this time of year. If started in the spring they will be larger, stronger plants to stand the winter, and their blooms may be larger the next season. But in the springtime we are usually too busy with our annuals to give any care to perennials, and the latter part of July, or the first of August, there are usually cloudy, moist days that give us again almost the conditions that we had for the spring seedlings. Nature is sowing many of her seeds now, for some have ripened, and even in your garden you may find tiny seedlings starting close by the mother plant. The seedlings that come up most quickly of themselves are often found beneath the shelter of a large leaf which has protected them from too hot a sun; and if there is one special thing that seeds need at this time of year in case the sunshine is hot and the air dry, it is a protection of lath or newspaper until they are fairly started. Give them water twice a day unless it rains. August is just the time to sow pansy seed, and thus get strong, early blooming plants for another season. Sweet Williams and foxgloves are easily raised at this time of year.

XIV

THE HARVEST

Then came the Autumn, all in yellow clad,
As though he joyed in his plenteous store,
Laden with fruits that made him laugh, full glad
That he had banished hunger. . . .
And in his hand a sickle he did hold,
To reap the ripened fruits the which the earth had yold.
Spenser.

CHAPTER XIV

THE HARVEST

THE harvest is your reward. Yet it is not all play. It is serious though enjoyable work to gather the crops and dispose of them in the best way. The harvest begins as soon as there is anything ripe to gather, and that happens all along, though the abundance comes in the fall of the year when the farmers gather the fruit of their season's labor.

The harvesting of flowers is an enjoyable study in arrangement of color, line, and texture. Ofttimes a single flower in a vase gives us more enjoyment than a mass of flowers, because then we see all the beauty of stem and leaf and the shape and color in each petal. Though we usually prefer a delicate blending of color in a bouquet, sometimes our color thirst is quenched

143

by a wild blaze of color and plenty of green foliage to blend it. Such a combination may be had with zinnias and mignonette. White sweet alyssum or candytuft often serves the same purpose in a bouquet that it does in the garden, sometimes encircling the bouquet, and sometimes mingling with it and blending the flowers. Have three kinds of vases for your flowers, — one tall and slender, another broad and shallow, and a third strong and large to hold a mass of flowers.

If flowers are to be marketed cut them in the cool hours of the early morning or else at night, and keep them in water. Do not cut flowers that are over-ripe. Poppies should be cut before they open, if used as cut flowers at all, because their petals fall so quickly. Protect cut flowers from strong light, unless they are such as need it to make them open.

In marketing vegetables remember, as we

THE REWARD OF THE HARVEST

said in the chapter on Spring Work, "As the early bird catches the worm, so the early market-gardener gets the price." An early crop is desirable, but a good crop at any time brings a good price, and quality should be considered more than quantity. Vegetables should be gathered in the early hours of the morning and delivered early in the day. They may be washed in cool water, and often some old dead leaves removed; but the root must sometimes be allowed to remain, as cutting it off causes the vegetable to lose some of the juices which make it palatable. This is especially true of beets. The roots of lettuce may be cut, leaving a good stem. Vegetables, when gathered, should be protected from the sun.

Both vegetables and flowers are usually at their best marketable stage for only a few days, and therefore a daily round of the garden is necessary for the market-gardener. Peas must

be nearly full size, yet tender and green. String
beans must not have developed to the point
when they become leathery and stringy. Beets
should be at least two and one half inches
through the widest part, unless they are sold
top and all when very small to be used as
greens.

Let me say right here that some vegetables
which grow wild and may not be marketable
are good wholesome food for the table. One
is that troublesome weed called " pusley." It
makes good greens, and in hot weather is much
better for us than many things. It needs plenty
of butter and salt and a little pepper mixed
with it when taken from the stove. Every one
knows the dandelion greens, and some know
that a delicious salad may be made from the
first fresh buds just as they start from the
ground in the springtime. Some people use
" lambs' quarters " and other of our wild vege-

tables, but it is never safe to use any excepting those which we thoroughly know.

Seed gathering may be considered a part of the harvest. Some people will say, "Never gather any seed. Buy it from the seedsman, who knows best how to raise it and gather it." This may be true of certain kinds of seed, and true of all seed if you buy of a first-class seedsman; but the seed gathered from your own garden often proves itself to have more vitality than seed bought at the stores. Only learn this: if you wish to save seed, save only a small quantity and only the best. Mark the plants that are well developed and of good quality. Remove the smaller, poorer blooms from them and gather only the best seed.

In harvesting, always gather everything that has ripened and dispose of it in some way. Make and keep the garden clean.

XV

IN THE YEARS TO COME

And still the constant earth renews
   Her treasured splendor; still unfold
   Petals of purple and of gold
Beneath the sunshine and the dews.

'T is God who breathes the triumph; He who wrought
   The tender curves, and laid the tints divine
Along the lovely lines; the Eternal Thought
   That troubles all our lives with wise design.

CELIA THAXTER.

CHAPTER XV

IN THE YEARS TO COME

PERHAPS this has been your first serious garden season with its successes and failures. Learn lessons from your failures and your successes alike. Both are stepping-stones to better things. All the time, I suppose, you have not forgotten the great world-garden of which yours is a part. If we all loved this God-given garden as we should, and cared for it, and thought and planned to keep it a beautiful place, how much we should do in the years to come to make our own little garden expand and help to start many another garden ! Plant life is so great a part of our life we cannot ignore it. We depend upon it for life. It clothes the earth in thousands of forms, to feed animals, to house men, to give pleasure, food, and raiment. When

151

LITTLE GARDENS

I hold a plant in my hand I hold a secret. Its secret of life I cannot guess. None can tell me. But I learn of its ways a thousand lessons, and I am satisfied.

Had you thought that this garden-work was only a pastime for the present? I hope not, for no matter what your work in life, you will do it better if you always keep one corner of your mind for the helpful friendship of a garden. There is no end to the pleasure to be found in a garden. It is a source of much knowledge and experience that will help you far beyond the garden's limits.

Aside from your garden, it is interesting to have a little plot for experimenting, for odds and ends, and for starting new things. Some people take great delight in making gardens for special purposes, herb gardens of quaint flavors and sweet odors, trial gardens of new varieties. It is a good plan to take one kind of plant, — the bean, for instance, — and see how many varieties you can raise, find their comparative value, and learn all you can about them both in books and through observation.

It may be you will find your life work among the plants, — as a market-gardener, a landscape-gardener or landscape-architect, a nurseryman, a seedsman, a florist, or as one of those few who go about helping boys and girls and everybody to make the world-garden stronger and brighter and more beautiful.

This one thing remember, — that if you wish to make a beautiful and useful garden, all the knowledge in the world, were it yours, would be of little use, if you were not willing to work hard at times, and to persevere daily in watching and caring for your plants. A daily round of the garden and a daily perseverance in fulfilling the needs of the day, however slight, are necessary. It is love and care that make a garden.

The Riverside Press
CAMBRIDGE . MASSACHUSETTS
U . S . A

CPSIA information can be obtained
at www.ICGtesting.com
Printed in the USA
LVHW041756150523
747056LV00013B/127